Love

Finale: Grown Woman Chronicles

Michelle Davis

Independently Published

Copyright © 2021 Michelle Davis

All rights reserved. No part of this publication may be reproduced, stored in, or introduced into a retrieval system, or transmitted, in any form or by any means, electronic, mechanical, photocopying, recording, or otherwise without the prior written consent of the copyright owner.

ISBN: 978-1-954613-00-3

Cover Art by: SelfPubBookCovers.com/ RLSather

Table of Contents

What is Love?	1
Love Song	2
I never knew	4
I Do	6
My Man	8
Climatic Love	10
The Key to Me	12
You See Me	14
Nobody's Perfect	15
Real	17
Love Pact	18
Reflection	19
Moments	20
For Us	22
Better	24

Glance	26
Raw honey	28
Seed	30
Anniversary	31
Blessing of You	33
Waited	35
Your Love	36
Finale	38

Introduction

The book title says it is the finale, but it is really the beginning of a beautiful journey of *Love* and acceptance. If you have read the other books in the *Grown Woman Chronicles* series, you will understand why this book is an exhalation; a long, slow deep breath.

My journey to love, both self and romantic, has taught me so much about the power of forgiveness. Love is not perfect and will never be perfect. The imperfections and acknowledgment of the possibilities and experiences of being in a state of love are the most beautiful aspects of loving.

Deep it in, the prequel, was full of drama, heartbreak, fear, uncertainty, lies, cheating, and immaturity. In the book *Over it!* I realized what I was experiencing and allowing myself to endure was not love, and enough was enough. The ending of the book *Over it!* was the beginning of self-love and true romance.

When the Mirror Spoke Back was my time in reflection, meditation, and prayer. Putting in the work to understand love, how to love, and receive love.

My goal with this book series was to share experiences and lessons learned. Bad experiences are not to break us, but are a wake-up call that we are not making the right choices, are on the wrong path, or simply need to make a change.

Growth is needed in life, and sometimes the lesson comes unexpectedly. Receive the lesson, reflect on it, grow from it, and come out better from having the experience.

The last book in the *Grown Woman Chronicles* poetry series is about *Love*. This book is about committed, unconditional, and mature love. Love is not a buzz word, not about flowers, jewelry, sex, trips, and Valentine's day. Love is an action, a devotion, a daily commitment that takes knowing and loving yourself. Hence, you are capable of loving someone else.

I hope you enjoy this book. Twenty years of living, learning, growing, realizing, maturing, accepting, and loving.

May your days be filled with happiness, reflection, growth, and LOVE!

Michelle Davis

What is Love?

A word we place with so much pressure and focus
Needing to hear it spoken
Validation of a feeling or emotion
Love
It means so much to many
Got to have
Really want it
Can't live without it
Lonely, sad, and depressed
In a place of despair
All I need is to hear those words
Spoken without thought it can be dangerous
Put things in motion
Love is a feeling rooted in authenticity and humility
Use your words carefully; use the word love responsibly

Love Song

I never understood the despair in a love song
The strained voice and cracked notes as the singer belted out words; conjuring memories of past love, new love, breakups, and pain

I often wondered about the sincerity of the melodramatic lyrics

How could a person arouse such feelings of anger and devotion in another person?

It was all a cliché until I met you
Our magical moments, and sweet surrenders have left me with a song of my own

I understand the longing, needing, and wanting

I understand not being able to articulate feelings and emotions

I understand the impact of love on the body and senses, a physical acknowledgment of uncertainties and fears

You mean so much to me; sometimes, I can only express myself in tears

I feel your energy when you are not around

I feel your emotions when you are near

A consecration commencing from divine intervention

A universal connection

Not just about physical interaction, more than just affection
A rhythm
Melodic and full of passion
I feel it, the notes in the song
Our love are the lyrics
You are my love song

I never knew

I never knew until I met you
   True Love
After all I have been through
I am shocked my heart was able to open up
Glad I did not allow the pain to run amuck
In my mind
In my heart
Closing me off to a great love of my lifetime
Patience, you have so much
Kindness, you show me and others every day
You move in silence, no flash, no show
What isn't said is understood
#Teamtogether
You want to see me win
Not just my lover, you are my best friend
For life

Yeah, committed

Breaking up is no dice

True Love

Matched by God and the angels above

Specially made, retrofitted

With you by my side, there is no limit

What we can do, what we can achieve

Ready to grow

Ready to live out dreams

Ready to love you wholeheartedly

Ready to give you all of me

I Do

The morning of our special day
    I rose early, gave God the glory
Gave thanks for all He had done
Waking me up, letting me see a new day
Getting me to my wedding day
I acknowledged the blessing He bestowed on me, on us
All the desires of my heart He provided
As I cried through the pain
My God knew I was ready, done with the games
Growth
I had done the work
Taking time out for myself
My solitude gave way to daily devotions and rejected notions of loneliness
Never lonely, but alone
I learned how to sing my own song

Leaned into my beauty
Understood my worth
Ruby
Flaws and all, the way God created
Imperfect poised for a purpose
Love, and the human experience
Changed
My inner lady is a grown woman
Ring on my finger
Standing at the altar
Past behind me
My future beside me
I said yes, hell yes, absolutely
I Do

My Man

When I look into your eyes, I see all of me
The me I am not always able to see
My past no longer matters, the present is all I need
You are my protector, my lover, and after God, and myself….my everything
Our love is enigmatic
No one could possibly understand
How I can spend my days, nights, and the rest of my life happy merely holding your hand
True deep abiding love
Our love is spiritual, otherworldly, futuristic, everlasting, often surpassing the need to be explained or defined
You are to me what the hand is to the arm, the foot to the leg, the neck to the head
Beautiful in design, your flaws are the perfect

addition to your unique existence

Love of my life, you speak to my heart in a language
only I can understand

Our meeting was by chance, not part of my plan

I am claiming you as mine, you are officially my man

Climatic Love

To know your heart before
    To know your heart after
After the love begins, before the first words are spoken
To feel your uncertainties
To feel your pain
Finishing sentences and thoughts
Enjoying the smell of rain
The calmness of our interaction
The excitement of our beating hearts
The mystery of thunder
The calm after the storm
To know your love without speaking; the words, your touch, the look on your face
Deep longing stares
Our bodies ignite in a ferocious flame

Our passion burns bright like a warm summer day

Hot

Deep

Cataclysmic

We are falling in love

The Key to Me

The key to me is you
    I thought you always knew
The way I keep you close
You are the one I love the most
The way I stare
Catching you unaware
Standing by my side
No one can fill your space
You are the only one who holds that place
In my heart
In my world
In my life
In my thoughts
No one else got that far
No matter how hard they tried
For me, it will always be you

I hope you feel this way too

You are a part of me

You are the key to me

You See Me

You see me like no one ever has
   You don't judge
You allow me to stretch out
You allow me to be in my emotions
You allow me the freedom to explore
The freedom to feel
You accept me
All of me
That's deep

Nobody's Perfect

Love is not perfect
I am glad we don't fake it
Real is what we are
That's the only way we are going to make it
My idiosyncrasies
Your ability to piss me off about little things
This is us
Some days you make me so mad, I yell and cuss
Mope and whine
Think about what it was like being single and who I
will marry in my next lifetime
It's selfish, I know, I can be selfish
You can be stubborn
The beauty is knowing.
No secrets, no lies
No hiding behind a mask or your representative

I know you, and you know me, and we decided in all our knowledge that we were meant to be

Real

My heart is an organ
My spirit is mystical
My soul is everlasting
Karma is real
I hear you when you are not speaking
I feel you when you are not around
Our connection has been established
This is real

Love Pact

I love you
    I shouldn't have to say it all the time
I live it
I breathe it
You are always on my mind
Don't you feel it when I enter into your space?
Your eyes light up
Your smile widens
There is joy all over your face
I love you
It doesn't get any better than that
I feel you
Our two souls have a love pact

Reflection

Do you see me?
Look in the corner of the mirror
Yeah, that's me
Every time you see yourself, you should see me
We are bonded, connected
Three cord strand, rings on the fingers of our hands
Ambassadors for black love
Married for life
Partners, lovers, and best friends
Tethered together, this is not a race
We need to find our cadence, maintain a steady pace
Teammates
Remember me every time you look at your face
I am a reflection of your love, a reflection of God's grace

Moments

We are going to have some moments when we want to be apart
Separate, get some space
Figure out who we are
It's ok
It's part of life
It's our spirits' way of getting respite so we can grow, sow, and keep moving forward
Taking a beat, taking a pause, a break is natural
Our relationship progresses when moments are taken and reflection occurs
No need to panic
This is love
Taking a moment, figuring things out will help move us forward
Please don't doubt

The process of thinking, being human

Individuality is not lost because we have a life partnership

The best in you needs the best in me to show up

Best…not perfection

Based on growth, maturation, and reflection

Take your time, relax, and unwind

Love yourself

Take this moment to gather your thoughts

I am here, no drama, patiently waiting

Don't rush

I need you to have this moment, as it is good for both of us

For Us

What is meant for you and me is not for everyone to know and see
No one else needs to know our business and what we do
No sharing, no venting to other people
Giving you bad advice, with an agenda I can see through
Our marriage, our commitment, our disagreements, our resolutions
What you say and what you did is biased
What I said and what I did is your own perception
Stop playing the victim and seeking alliances
I am not your enemy, don't ever make that mistake
Be careful who you talk to, be cautious of the snakes
Our "good thing" will have moments of confusion
Let's not get caught up in the illusion

Love is not perfect

Love is also not blind

Love understands there will be some difficult times

Moments of frustration

Ups and downs

Never separation

No loss of love

I am still with you

I want you to know this relationship is not for three, only two

Better

You teach me
I teach you
You believe in me
I believe in you
Truth
No matter how bad it sounds
Give it to each other straight
No battleground
Come from a place of love and care
Never catch you off guard
Always want you to be aware
When you are good
When you are great
When you are wrong
When you are making a mistake
Truth

Shouldn't have to lie

I got your back

I will be by your side

Support

I will always keep it real

Honesty and truth are a part of this deal

Marriage

The bringing together of two is more than saying the words, "I love you"

Together forever, we are still growing

We must be honest about the seeds we are sowing

The future

Mine

Yours

Ours

Let's work together

Have the tough conversations

Let's support each other

Let's make each other better

Glance

Across the room
Over the way
A little to the side with a smile
No matter how near or far
You always got me
Can pick me out like a shining star
You see me
Can't keep your eyes off me
Staring
Those warm large brown eyes
Always in your peripheral
Staying close
Our vibration guides you
The energy makes my heart swoon
Our connection is so infectious
No touch needed

No words to say

I see you

You see me

I feel you

You feel me

In this big world full of noise

Near, far, open-air, moon, and stars

The energy is fire between the two of us

Stop glancing at me, you are making me blush

Raw honey

No inhibitions, freedom
In a state of rawness; bare

Feeling every sensation in your body
Primal erotica
Synchronization of movement

Each bend, slant, or jarring motion
The element of surprise, both big and strong

Hard and smooth

Versatile and flexible textures working in tandem, creating stature and girth

An open bloom fortified by walls of silk lead to a

tunnel of liquid gold.

Hard and smooth meets the open bloom

Gyrations and penetrations engulf the room

The ride is slow, smooth, and melodic

As the bloom opens, the honey starts to flow

The hard and smooth texture swells in response to the pressure

Intensity beyond measure the hard becomes soft

Breathing heavily, satisfaction is sweet

Seed

You + me + baby
    Makes life worthwhile

Our little one

Blessed to us by God

Heir

Legacy

Part you, part me

A combination of the greatest parts of us

Your smile

My eyes

Your wit

My determination and grit

Our child, God's gift

A spiritual embodiment of our love

I look at you, look at him, and see the depths of God's grace for us

Anniversary

Another year
We made it through

Me and you

Together we grew

In Love

Maturation

Accountability

Responsibility

For each other's heart

Our marriage

Future

Family

We fought each day

Laughed and loved

Cried and prayed

Most importantly, together, we stayed

In it for the love of you

Hey, let this love flow through

Together forever

Thick and thin

Through it all, we have love

Blessing of You

What did I do to get blessed with you?
I have been through a lot
Many ups and downs
Heartache
Heartbreak
Disappointments
Sadness
I wrote it all down
Purged my soul
Face to the ground
Hands in the air
Praying, hoping someone made just for me was out there
Face to the ground, on my knees
I prayed to God to send me a good man or no man at all

Bless me with a partner, someone I can lean on
Hold me up
Catch me before I fall
Have great conversations
Travel and see the world
Get married, have a little boy or little girl
Snuggle at night, hold each other tight
Walk hand in hand, discussing our future, and making plans
I desired you and this type of love
I prayed fervently to the Lord above
I am grateful that he sent you to me
I was faithful; I knew God's love for me
I am humbled that he chose you to bless me

Waited

If I would have known true love was like this
I would have waited
Stayed at home and never dated
Sent a smoke signal for you to find
Focused on myself and plans for us
Learned how to cook
Read more books
Spent more time focused on me
Focused more on the type of person, wife, and mate I desired to be
Luckily for us, we secretly knew
You were for me, and I was for you
No regrets
All the detours, experiences of the past
Brought us together, lessons learned so our love could last

Your Love

Your love allows me to love
   Release fear
Practice patience
Be understanding
Sashay
Live with an open heart
Healing preceded our meeting
I am love and light
Free from pain
Living my life
Learned how to laugh and dance in the rain
Ready to start anew
Ready to go on a journey with you
Your love allows me to be myself
Feel me
Exist in a place of peace

Figuring out life with you
Making plans for us
Companionship
Not focused on the misguided secular expectations of relationships
Love
Simply, Love

Finale

I used to say, **What's Love?**
Love, Love, Love
Now, I have a **Love Song** of my own
True love, **I never knew** until I met you
Your patience, devotion, and sincerity, I had no issues saying **"I Do"**
I am your woman, and you are **My Man**
We have a **Climatic Love**
You See Me, you love me, you are the **Key to Me**
Nobody's Perfect, but I think what we have is **Real**
That is why I set the date, bought the dress, walked down the aisle, and sealed the deal
We made a **Love Pact,** together forever
Constant **Reflection** about our journey and how we are constantly growing
We know we will have **Moments** where we lose our

way

Focused and committed is how we need to stay

Mindful, this love is not platonic

A relationship for two, only **For Us**, just me and you

The good times and the "bad" will only make us

Better

I love all it takes is a smile and **Glance** to get back our romance

Raw Honey planted the **Seed** of a new life

Our son was born, a miracle, a true blessing

Part of you, and part of me

What else does our future hold, I can't wait to see it?

Until that time, let's celebrate every day like it's our

Anniversary

Toasting to love, toasting to trust, toasting to commitment and matrimony

A three-cord strand, rings on our fingers, hand in hand

Thanking God for seeing us through, thankful to God for the **Blessing of You**

Our romance was fated, etched in our book of life, glad I never gave up

Glad I **Waited**

For *Your Love*, Our Love, Simply, Love

www.ingramcontent.com/pod-product-compliance
Lightning Source LLC
Chambersburg PA
CBHW061304040426
42444CB00010B/2504

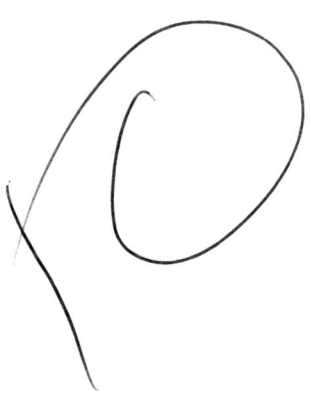

De Sibas

Notice historique sur M. de
Sibas, chef de bataillon en
retraite, à Mauléon, Basses-
Pyrénées (Éd.1846)